D0710342

A Note to Parents and Caregivers:

Read-it! Joke Books are for children who are moving ahead on the amazing road to reading. These fun books support the acquisition and extension of reading skills as well as a love of books.

Published by the same company that produces *Read-it!* Readers, these books introduce the question/answer and dialogue patterns that help children expand their thinking about language structure and book formats.

When sharing joke books with a child, read in short stretches. Pause often to talk about the meaning of the jokes. The question/answer and dialogue formats work well for this purpose and provide an opportunity to talk about the language and meaning of the jokes. Have the child turn the pages and point to the pictures and familiar words. When you read the jokes, have fun creating the voices of characters or emphasizing some important words. Be sure to reread favorite jokes.

There is no right or wrong way to share books with children. Find time to read with your child, and pass on the legacy of literacy.

Adria F. Klein, Ph.D.
Professor Emeritus
California State University
San Bernardino, California

Managing Editors: Bob Temple, Catherine Neitge
Creative Director: Terri Foley
Editors: Jerry Ruff, Christianne Jones
Designer: Les Tranby
Page production: Picture Window Books
The illustrations in this book were rendered digitally.

Picture Window Books
5115 Excelsior Boulevard
Suite 232
Minneapolis, MN 55416
877-845-8392
www.picturewindowbooks.com

Printed in the United States of America.

Library of Congress Cataloging-in-Publication Data
Moore, Mark, 1947-
Creepy crawlers : a book of bug jokes / by Mark Moore ;
illustrated by Anne Haberstroh.
p. cm. — (Read-it! joke books—supercharged!)
ISBN 1-4048-0627-X
1. Insects—Juvenile humor. 2. Wit and humor, Juvenile.
I. Title. II. Series.

PN6231.I56M66 2004
818'.602—dc22   2004007323

Creepy Crawlers

A Book of Bug Jokes

By Mark Moore • Illustrated by Anne Haberstroh

Reading Advisers:
Adria F. Klein, Ph.D.
Professor Emeritus, California State University
San Bernardino, California

Susan Kesselring, M.A., Literacy Educator
Rosemount-Apple Valley-Eagan (Minnesota) School District

PICTURE WINDOW BOOKS
Minneapolis, Minnesota

How is a fly swatter
like a baseball bat?

They both hit flies.

What insects are found in clocks?

Ticks.

What do you say to get rid of gnats?

Bug off!

Which bugs are the messiest?

Litterbugs.

When do bedbugs get married?

In the spring.

What do you call a fancy insect dance party?

A moth-ball.

What happens to beekeepers?

They get hives.

Which insects do well in school?

Spelling bees.

What's the name for a
musical insect?

A hum-bug.

What does an official say to
start a firefly race?

"Ready, set, glow!"

What do you get when you cross
an insect with a rabbit?

Bugs Bunny.

What bees are the hardest
to understand?

> *Mumble-bees.*

Which dance do insects prefer?

> *The jitterbug.*

Why do spiders spin webs?

> *Because they can't knit.*

What did the grasshopper general
say to his troops?

> *"Hop to!"*

Which insects tell time?

Clock-roaches.

Why do mosquitoes hum?

*Because they don't
know the words.*

How do you revive a moth?

*By using moth-to-moth
resuscitation.*

How do bugs send messages?

By flea-mail.

Where do bees wait for a ride
to school?

> *At the buzz stop.*

Which insects do battle
with knights?

> *Dragonflies.*

How was the spider's secret
plan discovered?

> *His phone was bugged.*

Which insects are famous
for building?

Carpenter ants.

What is a mosquito's
favorite sport?

>Skin diving.

What's worse than a shark
with a toothache?

>A centipede with
>athlete's foot.

What's the best transportation
for infant insects?

>A baby buggy.

Where do spider's get married?

>At a webbing.

What do you call an ant that lives with your uncle?

Your ant-y.

What language do ticks speak?

Tick talk.

Overheard at a spelling bee-hive:

RUAB2?ICUR.

Why did the baby firefly get a prize at school?

Because he was so bright for his age.

What wears spikes, has 18 legs, and catches flies?

A baseball team.

Which insects are known for their good manners?

Lady-bugs.

15

How did the flower get rid of the bee?

She told him to buzz off.

What do you call an ant that turns 100 years old?

An ant-ique.

Where should you look for bucking broncos?

Among horseflies.

What makes ticks so loyal?

When they make new friends, they really stick to them.

What was the largest
prehistoric moth?

The mam-moth.

What was the caterpillar's New Year's resolution?

To turn over a new leaf.

What insect takes photographs?

A shutterbug.

Which insect is famous for not being able to make up its mind?

The may-bee.

Why was the young ant
so confused?

> *Because all of his*
> *ants were uncles.*

Where do insects go to buy and
sell things?

> *The flea market.*

What do bees call their sweethearts?

> *Honey.*

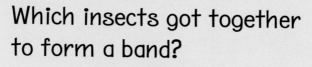

Which insects got together to form a band?

The Beetles.

Which insects sleep the most?

Bedbugs.

What insects do firefighters
battle most often?

Fireflies.

How do wasps communicate?

By bee-mail.

What do spiders like with
their hamburgers?

French flies.

How do you search for
a missing mosquito?

Start from scratch.

How does a centipede count
to 100?

On his feet.

Why don't ants ever get sick?

*Because they have
anty-bodies.*

What do you get when you
eat caterpillars?

Butterflies in your stomach.

What do bees use to brush
their hair?

Honey-combs.

What kind of music do
grasshoppers like?

Hip-hop.

Look for all of the books in this series:

Read-it! Joke Books—Supercharged!

Read-it! Joke Books